Instructions for Waking

Instructions for Waking

Poems by

Jennifer A. Hartenburg

© 2026 Jennifer A. Hartenburg. All rights reserved.
This material may not be reproduced in any form, published,
reprinted, recorded, performed, broadcast,
rewritten or redistributed without
the explicit permission of Jennifer A. Hartenburg.
All such actions are strictly prohibited by law.

Cover design by Shay Culligan
Cover image by Engin Akyurt and Meghan Larkin on Unsplash
Author photo by Christian Webster, Webster Media Houston,
www.webstermediahouston.com

ISBN: 978-1-63980-846-5
Library of Congress Control Number: 2026931539

Kelsay Books
502 South 1040 East, A-119
American Fork, Utah 84003
Kelsaybooks.com

for G.H.

Acknowledgments

Thank you to the following publications, in which versions of these poems previously appeared.

The Christian Century: "Kierkegaard's Canary"

Dappled Things: "Instructions for Waking"

Rattle: Poets Respond: "Houston is the body"

The Saint Katherine Review: "Tango Botánico"

Weber: The Contemporary West: "Deciduous," "Our Lady of Wooden Comfort"

Additional Praise for *Instructions for Waking*

Jen Hartenburg's *Instructions for Waking* is an allusive and luminous collection that builds bridges between art and nature. These poems are tender, searching, and intellectually alert—they invite the reader to contemplate questions of philosophy, love, fertility, and the divine. With language capable of both soothing and surprising, Hartenburg fearlessly lays bare the mystic connection that pulses between the inner life and the living world.

—Bethany Getz, Author published in *Windhover,* the *Saint Katherine Review,* and the *Imaginative Conservative.*

Instructions for Waking explores the fullness of language and experience, and in echoes equal parts Gerard Manley Hopkins and Mary Oliver, beautifully marries the two. Through a stunning array of evocative imagery, illuminating puns, philosophical nods, and pregnant allusions, Hartenburg reminds us of the power of words, bringing to bear both their earthy and ethereal aspects on our inner and outer realities. In so doing, this collection effects a satisfying reproachment between the natural and the personal, the objective and subjective, the mythological and the intimate. One can never quite reach the depths of these surprisingly accessible poems, which is just as well. They demand and deserve revisiting, with each encounter introducing us anew to ourselves and our world. Time with them is time well-spent.

—Marybeth Baggett, Co-author of *Telling Tales*

As its title suggests, the poems in *Instructions for Waking* both teach and delight, inviting the reader to admire rachis and down, mud and rivulet, squelch and sparkle. Filled with coarse crumbs of forgiving and living earth, here is sustenance for lovers of words and of nature. Hartenburg's attention to sound, syllable, and form demonstrates her range as a poet, and the order and design within these poems, deserving of slow enjoyment, is matched with adventure: There is plenty to discover in her lexical layers and turns, and vistas varying from Mt. Athos to Pascagoula. Often spiritual and maternal in their watchfulness, here are poems about birth and death, the sacred in the soil and wind. These poems will stir and reward the student of word, image, and thought.

—Emily E. Stelzer, Author of *Gluttony and Gratitude: Milton's Philosophy of Eating*

Contents

Part 1: Strange Birds

Aubade with Palpitations: At Sunrise I Recall My Death	17
Bull Riding, February 11, 1963	18
Kierkegaard's Canary	19
Our Lady of Wooden Comfort	20
Found Blood Moon	21
Strange Birds	22
Elegy for a Blackbird	23

Part 2: What Thrushes Wing There

Deciduous	27
Instructions for Waking	28
Sunday After Pentecost	31
Black-Bellied Whistling Duck	33
Learning Greek	34
Persephone Home for Spring Break, Demeter Talks Herself Down	35
Eve and Her Daughters: A Genealogy Transposed	36
Hair is its own calligraphy	40

Part 3: Hundred-Feathered Love Song

Toward Earth	43
Tango Botánico	44
Houston is the body	46
Turtle Fountain	48
The Marriage of Poetry & Philosophy	50

Zeal	53
Ars Poetica	54
Hundred-Feathered Love Song	55
Notes	67

Part 1: Strange Birds

Then he sent out a raven, which kept going to and fro until the waters had dried up from the earth.

—Genesis 8:7, NKJV

Aubade with Palpitations:
At Sunrise I Recall My Death

Your song sounds an alarm, little grackle, dear heart.
Your stuttering "chitip" agitates the weighted air.
The sky flares the color of blood and red agate
against the cramped wing-barrel dark.

Your stuttering "chitip" agitates the weighted air.
Your ink-damp, oil slick of feathers thuds
against the cramped wing-barrel dark
within this cage of ribs.

Your ink-damp, oil slick of feathers thuds
away what's left of sleep.
Within this cage of ribs
your shrill "reedle-eek" rises.

What was left of sleep
alarmed the sky. Little grackle, bird heart,
raise your shrill "reedle-eek" now—
your song the color of blood-red agate.

Bull Riding, February 11, 1963

> *The bull surged up, the bull surged down,*
> *Not to be stayed by a daisy chain*
> *Nor by any learned man.*
>   —Sylvia Plath, "The Bull of Bendylaw"

When Sylvia rode that black bull down,
she shot right out of the bucking shoot

with no sickly resolution
only action—exits sealed,

glove rosined, the gate-door hinged
wide at her nod. She spurred the bull-

snouted beast, her long-time companion,
for the short-go, her controlled

flailing finally in rhythm with
the bucking bull's belly rolls

with the heaving waves of its drops
and kicks, its dizzy spinning rounds.

She rode the full eight seconds and more
before she let go her grip

let slip the braided bull rope and the bell
dropped to the sand. She'd stay her stay no more.

Kierkegaard's Canary

and freedom looks down into its own possibility,
laying hold of finiteness to support itself
   —Vigilius Haufniensis, "The Watchman" of Copenhagen,
   The Concept of Anxiety

Kierkegaard's canary was happy
as a lark until Kierkegaard set

it free. Now the whole bright world
spins out beneath its flight, its heart
in palpitations. Yes; the whole

bright glorious world spins,
the whole bright, blinding world.

Our Lady of Wooden Comfort

Virgin and Child, Northern France,
early to mid-fourteenth century, wood
The Menil Collection, Houston

Just here beside pale Cycladic
figures and Coptic tapestry
transposed from other age and place

she spreads her giddy grin open-
mouthed across a youthful wooden
face, her arms lovingly embrace

a headless Christ. Her hips are thrust
upward to bear the Child's weight.
Her belly rises plump and round

under carved folds of gown, and down
her middle runs a rift that rends
breast from breast—linea nigra

in negative space, scar from time's
scalpel having as it were pierced
her heart and side, lancet through which

her God has sprung half-formed yet full
of favor, fingers folded, hand
held in heedful benediction.

Time-rent she smiles seeing still
the face beyond our knowing.

Found Blood Moon

Sky & Telescope livestream, September 27, 2015

Totality has begun.
Now completely inside the dark
core of earth's shadow the face
of the moon should be wholly
obscured but sunlight *refracting*

round the edges of atmosphere
leaks into the shadow—watch
the colors suddenly change
here—hints of blue and green amid
the red—Rayleigh scattering.

So this is what we talk about
as the view grows unwontedly
dim: the *long, glancing path* of light.

Strange Birds

A dart of blue against the blue
and brown of winter branches
entwined with sky, a jay bird lights
upon the fence, cocks jaunty
cobalt head, and eyes me.

A goldfinch makes his southward flight,
one turn of his migration.
A gleam, a glint, a clinquant hint,
a flash in December's lockpan,
he will molt, fly north again.

The cardinal in the naked shrub
makes a brash flirtation.
A sudden crimson in the tree,
a branch ablaze but not consumed—
brief flame and then a vacuum.

A reel of color out-of-reach,
bright, alive, elusive—
Yet I am Eve regenerate
sighting among the ashes
new strange and feral graces.

Elegy for a Blackbird

When I found your figure underneath the cypress glutting
black ants with your eyeballs, you were slick of mud-caked
    feathers,
bone frame, beak. I thought to bury you, my little grackle, but
you were doing such good work there nourishing the others.

Living, you were always slutting yourself out to every
birdbrained choir, always shrieking, carrying on, and voicing
all your pleasures and concerns, and crying out, *"Pas chére!*

Pas chére!" Now your head space tends the other, and your riven
chest is widened. Freed from that proclivity toward smallness,
you will now expand, become a blessing—gift of dust.

Part 2: What Thrushes Wing There

mi ritrovai per una selva oscura

—Dante, *Inferno*

At 20 weeks, a female fetus has a fully developed reproductive system, replete with six to seven million eggs.

—Lexi Krock, "Fertility Throughout Life," *PBS*

Deciduous

As with most things in life, when planting, say,
a trumpet creeper underneath the oak,
it's best if you don't second-guess yourself.
Perhaps you will, through lack of expertise,
at last choke out its life just as you fear.
May be your dearth of knowledge as regards
the "dripline" and the "critical radius"
leaves you surprised to find the bulk of roots
wound through the top three feet of soil. It will
not do you good this late to read that white
oak's known to be "sensitive to severance."
Those inelegant strokes of your shovel have
already stripped small dark veins down to pale
cream-white marrows. Pick up your spade and finish.

Get down on knees and gloves and reconcile
yourself to clay. Roughen the root ball, now
fill in, and tamp down. The garden may yet survive,
profuse in orange-red blossoms, also acorns.

Instructions for Waking

after reading Mary Oliver

You will not long remember
which part is dream and
which is waking parable.
Having filled your head
with American poems—
Virgilian guides—you've
waded into sleep's black wood
a more primitive
you crashing through

                         the tangled
ripe undergrowth. Who
can say what thrushes wing there,
what honeyed berries
swell wild in the bush, what
litanies, what rites?
As dawn returns, you
return more nearly to your
self, growing, perhaps,

more conscious of your children
sleeping lightly now
nearby. Light laps like water
along the shore where
you know what you must do, what
herculean feat.
Now at the frozen mountain
lake that is your life,
you take

                a mammoth hammer
so large you cannot
wield it—and poise it even
so above your head.
Bearing down with force, you smash
the white glistening
plane, opaque and lovely, but
not before the ice,
hexagons expanding, cracks

the dam you did not
know was there. The crystal slabs
of all that floating
ice refracting light in each
direction will blind
you. Dizzy you will fall down
and under water.
You may wonder then whether
and which way

                    to swim,
the press of searing
water constricting you on
every side. Perhaps
you will fight the flow a while,
limbs frogging toward
the surface, a warmer more
familiar light, lungs
burning. It

                    doesn't matter.
You will not ever
breathe again—not like that. Pray
for gills. Fighting, or
no, you will come to the lip
of the lake, crowning
round out the breach in the dam.
You might slip-slide straight
through, or the water

                              may squeeze
for hours nudging
inch by slow inch, but sooner
or later you will
emerge from your tense matrix
to find yourself flung
wide and spilling down mountains
in the roaring stream.
Bruised, you will come

                              to cliff fall
after cliff fall, swan
diving ever down and down,
eternally drowned.
Looking about, you will see
gilled angels splitting
the water, leaping in spasms
of wonder at
                    your side

Sunday After Pentecost

Chora, Serifos, June 19, 2022

There is too much   wind, and too much
noise. The gale-force   gusts sound shudders
through the scoured   shell of this modest
byzantine cathedral   balanced at the crest
of the island rise.   Inside, the sparse
collection of   congregants stay
or stir: a handful   of snow-haired
men are tending   beeswax tapers
or intoning each   in turn; a woman
leans an arm   and listens, inclines
her head of greying   curly hair.
A few others   fringe the edges
and stand or sit   in shadowed seats.

A young child,   a girl, her cheeks
and forehead   framed in shocks
of short black hair,   moves blithely,
without ceasing,   with senses wide.
At times I catch her   considering me.

Hello, bright eyes.   What must this bonnie
think of me?   Does she marvel
at me straggling   here, a stranger
from half a world   away? And why
am I *here* inside   this hill-top temple?
An ill-timed traveler,   I'm too tardy.
I have missed   the mystic moment.

There is bread given   instead of the gifts,
a blessing of sorts.   I stay to note

the flares of saints that fill each surface
of exposed space from base to ceiling.
Candles in sand— filled stands flicker
still radiant, regardless of squalls.

While the cantors continue wielding
familiar tones in unfamiliar
tongue. I hum the tune but have
lost the words. In other-worldly
artwork above the altar screen,
stunned apostles sit as descending
streaks of fire enflame their souls
loose their lips with every language.

Someone collects the candle stubs,
turns out the lights. I take the hint.
I've come too late and lingered too long.

The small blessing of bread snugged
within my fingers, I furl myself
into the rush and roil of wind.

Black-Bellied Whistling Duck

For a whistling duck,
belly more buoyant than head,
spring takeoff is rough.

Learning Greek

My mouth is ocean, tide of tongue
tapping islands of teeth, tannic
words sighing against the breakers.
My lips curve on bends of pebbled
syllables—unfamiliar shores
of breath and sound and sibilance.

Motion of mouth becomes spark, tongue
fire. Ancient alphabet, fennel
and forethought of Prometheus,
sizzles and flames. Φτιάχνω[1] new
shapes with tongue and teeth, fashion hot-
breathed chains of susurrant phonemes.
My mouth is furnace, beacon, pyre.

Voice is the rush of wind in reeds,
flute and lyre, aspirates and rose-
round vowels. The dance of honeybees
is in my throat—more bumble now
than hymn, melisma, honeyed hum—
ἐλέησον[2] incessant on my lips.

---

1. *ftiachno:* "I make"
2. *eleison:* "have mercy"

Persephone Home for Spring Break,
Demeter Talks Herself Down

I speak to you silently now, daughter, while I watch you stand in the slanting sunlight watering the chrysanthemums. You comment on the pile of compost I've left oozing by the sink, offer to take it out for me. Forgive me my recent torrents. You move tall as a pine mast gliding out to the garden. Plaint of an eastern meadowlark lilts through the door: "See-you; see-you." The mums in the window boxes seem sated by the measured amount.

Eve and Her Daughters:
A Genealogy Transposed

Cycladic Islands, June 2022

I. Οικογένεια[3]

Deep in her body twin tips of goat
horns blossom, bouquet into lilac,
iris, and oleander. Between
the tines of the horns primordial
tides brim shores, fill and flow by season.
Warblers bewilder orchards, thicken
the fruit on weighted branches with song—
swollen abundance of apricots.

Leaves make poor cover and short shrift. Brooks
and rivers well and pulse through ancient
beds lined with veined stones silent as names
of forgotten faces. Bitterns wade,
surprise a stonepit, remains of fruit
tried too soon, now rolling in the wash.

---

3. Οικογένεια (*oikogéneia*): family, household, kin

II. Φυλή[4]

Deep in her body quail scuttle, chirp
like laughter escaping over sand
dunes. Aroma of singed goat—tent flap
lifts in the breeze. The reservoir spills
overwhelmed with the impossible.
The donkeys watered and home, low hills
electrify with coastal scrub, wild
capers. Dragons snap out of granite
cliffs and outcrops. Swifts dip their consent.

A bat sings its silence, haunts the crave
of night. Island caves echo at tide's
ebb, sigh to be filled—wet curves of bare
calcite, weak-eyed ache of cold and heat.

---

4. Φυλή (*phulé*): tribe, clan, contingent

III. Έθνος[5]

Deep in her body a cove dilates
like an osprey's eye, and sparrows blaze
out of a canyon—*too lively, too*
quick. Struck peaks open into fountains—
colostrum-tinged amber in the dawn.

Her body is a cord of scarlet,
a covering of fennel, escape
and promise, land of milk and honey.

Deep in her body iron lodes glint,
supply what comes to hand—a needle
and cookpot, hammer and spike. Sickle-
clawed falcon swoops from the blind of sun.

Her body is sheaves of gold seagrass
surprising feet on a threshing floor.

---

5. Έθνος (*éthnos*): nation, people, host

IV. Κόσμος[6]

Deep in her body current and wind
compass the circumference of coastline.
A kestrel hovers over footpath
and rose garden and unbreached terrain.

Her body is moor line and hitch, trawl
net and trawler, expanse of blue sea.

Deep in her body a cormorant
submerges for a count of forty—
within her own body, another
body—new orchards within orchards,
each small branch flush with song-ripened fruit.

---

6. Κόσμος (*kósmos*): world, universe, earth; order, form; adornment

Hair is its own calligraphy

its own ink and fluidity.
Curls write a loud subtext in text-
ure. Circuitous lines spring back,
resist expectations, provide
twists of definition. Each curl
is cue, headline, manifesto.
Here is a revel of ravel,
a crescendo coming to head.
Every length is a volume, lift
on its own terms in pop and peak.
Read in it *hairs poetica,*
each strand signed as large as Hancock.

Part 3: Hundred-Feathered Love Song

*Earth's the right place for love:
I don't know where it's likely to go better.*

—Robert Frost, "Birches"

Toward Earth

The way a squirrel
hangs down for seed,
the crepe tree bent
from sky toward earth,

calls to mind
a child I saw,
two full fists sunk
in the blessed bread bowl.

Tango Botánico

Awaking you, bee,
I'm awakened.
I'm your flower,
your honeycomb.
Production rises
like summer crops of
corn or basil
under skies of
   Nerudian
   turquoise.

Foxgloves reach up
high above us,
still we find ourselves
without shielding shade.
Our thirst drives us
to sit with silence,
to contemplate words,
to plead or give forth,
   perhaps to self-
   restrain.

We are careful
not to wake the
sleeping orchid,
his labellum
flanged, a milk-drunk
infant curling
tendril hands loose
    beneath
    his chin.

We tip-toe silent
past the crocus,
her petal eyes closed
in dreams of sparrows.
She sees them flitting—
    oh!—so
    brightly
    by.

Houston is the body

of your lover found flipped
in a car on the side
of the freeway. You weren't
there when it happened. You
were at home sheltering
from the storm, sheltering
at your breast the child who
is also Houston. *Shhh.*
Shhh. Shhh. Shhh. In your dreams
you are Houston watching
rain water pool 'round your
ankles. Paralysis
of sleep has bound you. There
is nowhere to go. You
wake shaking to the sounds
of your child crying.
You offer her your breast.
She will not latch. Her tears
now pool thick around your
doorways. Paralysis
of grief overtakes you.
They have taken your limp
lover to hospital.
You fear the worst. You dream
your bed a raft afloat,
a dinghy bobbing on
roads turned into rivers.

You peer over the edge
and see the face, the eyes
of your lover looking
back from the depths. You do
not wake because it is
not a dream. The phone rings.
It is your lover who
calls from the hospital:
"Get a pen," he says; "write
this down: *Houston is not
dead.*" The child is sleeping
a strand of your hair clenched
tight in her strong, fierce fist.

Turtle Fountain

Jewish Ghetto, Rome

Lu cuntu nun metti tempu.[7]

Midday in Piazza Mattei, light
unpolarized reflects off marble
and bronze where not three but four youths
shimmer fiery and fleet in the fountain.
Shrinking from the chill of January sun,
a passerby may barely take in the water.

Muzio Mattei was homesick for water;
that is why he contrived to lighten
his own piazza with the sunny
beauty of sculpted bronze and marble
finely crafted and formed into a fountain
removed from the ghetto market and its youths:

Resting a foot on a dolphin's head, each sculpted youth
grasps in hand the same dolphin's tail. Water
spouts from dolphins' mouths and falls to the fountain's
four shells and down again into the light-
colored basin below. Around the marble
vasque above, amorini pucker at the sun.

Once, the amorini, after the sun
had set, drew the four lithe, fine-chiseled youths
away through the ghetto streets marbled
silver and slate like deep sea water.
Each amorino aimed at the moon's light
three arrows tipped with flame fountaining

---

[7] Time takes no time in a story.

heavenward. Donna Luna, her eyes a fountain-
head, sent back spirits radiant with love to sun
the steel black stones—polar bodies lighting
here and here—a scattered gleaming of youthful
brass *stolpersteine* springing up to stay the water
of memory from spilling away like marbles.

When Mattei stumbled upon those stones, he marveled,
took his gate key, and threw it into the fountain.
To keep himself from gazing ever more into the waters,
he ordered his window closed off to the sun.
They say a brick-closed frame near the four youths
of bronze to this day shuts out the daylight.

The fountain's turtles were added after Mattei's light
had waned. Ever surmounting the marble lip, each youth-
like turtle stretches toward the live water and the sun.

The Marriage of Poetry & Philosophy

Wedding guests freed large flocks of words
some of which lifted and dropped in groups
to coo around flowers or flutter at sunsets.
Clusters settled on trees and traced
branches of various neat distinctions.

Poetry played coy, veiled in ambiguity.
Philosophy flexed a well-hewn clarity.
Bloom branch stem root
There were no words at the consummation—
each unraveled the other's logic;

both were breathless—a good beginning.
Clay water fire wind
Morning came and each began
to learn new ways to wield their words.
They tried out fresh and old positions

first one on top and then the other.
He delighted at her directness.
She pined—*Oh!*—for his digressions.
Plums apples oranges cherries
They played some tricks and stretched validity

then got steamy over soundness.
At times they fought over register,
syntax, matter and meter—the usual.
They flirted in puns and parentheticals,
threw their plates over "think" and "feel,"

made up panting over "know."
She puzzled out his syllogisms;
he plumbed all her metaphors.
Root stem branch bloom
In time they found they were expecting,

and they were fruitful again and again.
Apples oranges cherries plums
They carried many doubts to term,
lost and grieved some certainties.
The surviving brood were zesty, true,

demure and truculent in turns.
Seed swell catkin flower
Bride and groom held fast together,
Wandered down semantic lanes
through the years and library shelves.

Hunkered down to craft and pen,
weft and weave of ink and page,
they made and loved, and made love,
found wisdom spread in wrinkled lines
across the other's ancient face—

beauty more dear because opaque.
Wind fire water clay
At last the lovers died it seems.
(Neither could outlast the other.)
Mystics buried them side by side,

tucked them gently away in earth.
Catkin flower seed swell
Yet words winged out of their grave and flew—
a star-bright flock fluttering up
into the vast and singing sky.

Zeal

Jasmine swells over
the mailbox, reaches for more,
climbs on air: *Send me.*

Ars Poetica

> *you lay out a line . . . watching all the angles.*
> —Annie Dillard, *The Writing Life*

The line you first lay down falls flat, awry.
You find it slant, a bridge untethered, drowned.
You start off on another angle shy

of destination, attempt another vector,
yet the angles are all wrong, askance—
one too obtuse, another terribly

acute. No matter. You must still persist
in webbing out each wing, flinging wide
this net in which you catch yourself, angling

for stars. The snare's the only sure salvation.
You must reenter your papery nest
and find the center where all lines connect—

the spun dreamcatcher, cradle, eye of God.
You measure out the turns, find shape, or else
suggested shape—perhaps, drunk on your own

geometry, surprise yourself with shock
of symmetry, behold penumbra crossed
in bird-bone grids of unaccounted light.

Hundred-Feathered Love Song

I. Starling

> *Everyone has to build anew his sky.*
> —Kakuzo Okakura, *The Book of Tea*

The earth is a cradle suspended from the bough
of a pine tree tall and dark as the new moon, wrapped
in the heady smell of dry leaves dampened, heavy
with sod. Strange and lovely as hadrosaurs, black-bellied
ducks have sunk to the mirror-glass face of the lake.
Sunset spreads on the water, fractals of dimming
sky and silhouetted tree. Cicada song swells

electrifies the evening with the urgency
of first love. A flint grey ribbon of water winds
luminous through a dusk-dim bayou exhaling
into the gloaming. The earth paves a roadway through
the Milky Way as we lay down concrete over
the Pascagoula. We ride east all night, branches
of tupelo inking out stars on either side.

Our eyes strain to see the way with what light we have.
Shadows begin to separate themselves, detach
from the general darkness, liminal signals
of imminent dawn. A spattering of starlings
congeal on a wire. Phosphorus rises, trace
of amber above the black horizon. *Evening
and morning, one day.*

II. Bluebird

> *Birds of God, birds of joy [. . .]*
> *Am I not in paradise now?*
>   —Markel in *The Brothers Karamazov*

Scrub jay, kingfisher, blue-throated humming-
bird, blue heron, cerulean warbler.
The earth is the feather of a bluebird
spinning on its rachis. It's an infant's

first laugh. It's a sailcloth windmill whirling
in an aquamarine sky, a phthalo
of tree swallows circling in eternal
summer murmurations. Migration is

rotation is revolution is time.
Feel how the cradle rocks on solar wind.
Blue jay, bluebird, bluethroat thrush, indigo
bunting, peacock. For sheer exuberance

the common swift would fly up to the moon
and back seven times in the course of life
but instead measures its heaven-bound arc
across terrestrial continents. Such

is its capaciousness. It will make love
tumbling through the air entwined in a flash
of penetration. Northern parula,
blue-gray gnatcatcher, lazuli bunting,

grosbeak. We migrate in steel over these
asphalt lanes and mesquite-lined highways—each
cattle pond a microcosm of cloud
and cobalt. To the north, nimbostrati

drop iridescent scrim while you and I
slip with the road in and out of shadow—
cool cloud cover giving way in a warm
release of sunlight again and again

until we cannot say which pleases more,
the expectant darkness or just after.
Our exhalations escape, swallowtails
lifted over the hood in the headwind.

III. Yellow Flicker

> *In pursuit of old age and happiness, I follow the lightning*
> *and approach the place where it strikes.*
> —Diné Bahane'

The earth is a wizened turtle
bobbing in gold-flecked fountain froth.
It's a fat squirrel hanging upturned
in a myrtle, a quail coppered
by the down-sliding sun half sunk
beyond the willow, a sphinx moth
transfigured in a headlight beam.

Yellow flicker, sapsucker, great
kiskadee, waxwing, meadowlark.

Sun slips south toward Capricorn,
shines slant through autumn's honeyed lens,
diffuses across sweeps of rust-
tinged ash, copses of oaks wind-tossed
and glitter washed, a flare of bronze
and amber. We stagger beneath
sun-drunk trees feathered with Spanish
moss, backlit lace—fringe of snowy
egret bending to gilded creek.
The lengthening light weaves through leaves,
lies like latticework on buttered
grass, makes a halo of your hair.

Golden-crowned kinglet, tanager,
flycatcher, warbler, yellowthroat.

Slow tree roots ripple the pavement
the way our hands grope and hunger
beneath the other's clothes, buckling
and unbuckling. I open to you
the way the sky opens around
a bend in the road at the crest
of the hill—Abiquiu basin
spreads out below, a swell of mid-
autumn cottonwoods descanting
in ardent cadmiums, blazing
past windshield and rearview mirror—
our future and our past. The light
of the trees bores into the chest's
cavity, hordes a cache of fire-
yellow hearts flickering from each
dark branch of vein and artery.

Golden-crowned sparrow, canary-
winged parakeet, goldfinch, verdin.

October thunders, pounds heavy
wet rain on the glass. Even our
dreams are generative. You sleep
on my breast, your body corpselike,
slung across rumpled linen sheets,
half drowned in dreams of immortality.

Golden plover, western kingbird,
oriole, yellow-breasted chat.

We're not yet too wise and weary
To still be caught amazed. The sky,
still bright, not yet a dead, damp pigeon
wing, the sea not yet a raging bull.

IV. Northern Shrike

> *God showed me three nothings*
> —Julian of Norwich

The Milky Way roils,
hurricane spiraling
across the universe—
the earth in a rainband
spins out from the center.

My arms shield you against
the violence of sleep, its
sudden convulsive flights
and falls. Beyond the pane
cotton fields expand in
constellations of boll
and bract. A galaxy
of cattle egrets lifts
from ridge and furrow. Ridge
and furrow fold once more
into the earth, the run
concluding in order
to repeat. A white-tailed
deer slips into a gorge.

Cold presses and wraps limbs
in balsam and in bark,
armor for this season
of cessation. The earth
is white-breasted, a hawk
perched in a leafless birch.
The earth is a brittle
bough, withered breast, fallow
field, the orb of an eye
focused far beyond us.

The hand of the clock reaves
as it revolves. Mourning
doves moan like memory
in bare aspen branches
inked and resined across
pale clouded sky—cold-piqued
capillaries of lung
spread bronchiole and lobe
from the loam.
                Migration
and appropriation
are our constants. We leave
in order to return,

speak to repeat words said
before—shrikes silvering
the shortening days, we
revisit our hunger
impaled on a nettle.

Land and language carry
their ashes—every word
a borrowed artifact,
pattern rent from other
fabric. Silent letters
bare bones of forgotten
sounds.
        We enter the world
wordless, and we leave all
words behind. Every clod
of indifferent earth, each
sound resists all our claims.

Impervious to flag
or band, the land we've claimed

shall take and enfold us,
each appropriator
arrogated at last,
an appropriate end.

Nothing is mine. I hang
my heart on hummingbirds
and watch them fly away.
Flutter of nuthatches
in a leafless shrub sends
me reeling, backlit spears
of evergreen run me
through—an unmerited
death, beauty past desérts.

Grasping falters. Frail hands
release all that remains:
silence as of circling
volts of vultures, faint scent
of bodies on a sheet,
algid faith in the long
persistence of seed and
sap beneath the sod.

V. Painted Bunting

> "'Come with me,' said Fisher. 'We must jump up.'"
> —Anishinaabe starlore

Let these memories be eternal: peach blossoms of cloud
in a violet bowl of sky, blush of roseate spoonbills,
fountain of catkins, slick of rainbow in a grackle's sheen.
Now the earth is a new earth; it is a bee nectar-deep
in the throat of a sword lily. It's a bunting arcing
through the heavens, whorl alighting on a hand which catches
also the slivered moon, an afterfeather, a bright barb
of the cherubim. The newborn sun is an albatross

splitting open our horizon. It is a charm fashioned
from elytra and hind wings of every lucent beetle:
tiger, dogbane, and jewel. Light clips in syncopation
over the water and draws butterflies out of the sea—
Monarchs at the end of an impossible migration.
Every winged thing is rose-gilded in this dawning. Layered
valleys and hills interlace like lovers' fingers. Mountains
here will carve our hearts out, then wear them rust-red and jagged,

still beating, on sleeves of salmon and burnt umber strata.
A shoal of rose-ringed parakeets flares above a bumper
crop of pine cones. Cones encase piñons by the hundreds, pairs
catacombed in sealed chambers until the scale doors blister
open and fling wide the winged sleepers. Today peace is wild
thyme and fennel in flower. Every grain of sand singes,
and what we take for driftwood transmutes into a sudden
levity of wing and flight, herons startled into ascent.

Notes

"Toward Earth"
Blessed bread, also called *antidoron* or *eulogia*, is the bread offered at the end of the Orthodox Christian liturgy.

"Houston is the body"
This poem was written during Hurricane Harvey and its aftermath, August 2017.

"Turtle Fountain"
The epigraph is from a quotation which Italo Calvino includes in his work *Six Memos for the Next Millennium*.

Stolpersteine: Scattered throughout the ghetto and the surrounding city, two-hundred brass stones known as *stolpersteine* (German for "stumbling stones") commemorate one-tenth of the two-thousand Jews deported from Rome in 1943.

About the Author

Jennifer A. Hartenburg teaches writing and literature in the Houston area where she lives with her husband, two children, and two cats. She holds a B.A. in English and M.A. in Education, both from Biola University where she remains a perpetual member of the Torrey Honors College.

Her work has appeared in various publications including *Christian Century, Dappled Things, Rattle: Poets Respond, The Saint Katherine Review,* and *Weber: The Contemporary West.* Jen is continually rediscovering the power of word and world to startle and heal with beauty.

www.ingramcontent.com/pod-product-compliance
Lightning Source LLC
Chambersburg PA
CBHW030914170426
43193CB00009BA/845